CHOIR BUILDERS 2

FOR GROWING VOICES

24 MORE Vocal Exercises for Warm-Up & Workout

By Rollo Dilworth

TABLE OF CONTENTS

PLAYBACK+

Speed • Pitch • Balance • Loop

To access AUDIO MP3s, go to:
www.halleonard.com/mylibrary

Enter Code
1795-6946-3817-5552

ISBN: 978-1-4803-6412-7

HAL•LEONARD®

7777 W. BLUEMOUND RD. P.O. BOX 13819 MILWAUKEE, WI 53213

Visit Hal Leonard Online at
www.halleonard.com

Contact us:
Hal Leonard
7777 West Bluemound Road
Milwaukee, WI 53213
Email: info@halleonard.com

In Europe, contact:
Hal Leonard Europe Limited
42 Wigmore Street
Marylebone, London, W1U 2RN
Email: info@halleonardeurope.com

In Australia, contact:
Hal Leonard Australia Pty. Ltd.
4 Lentara Court
Cheltenham, Victoria, 3192 Australia
Email: info@halleonard.com.au

T0079483

CHIMES IN THREE-QUARTER TIME

TIP: The Voice Chime part (added on the repeat) should emulate the sound of bells by going immediately to the "ng" and also adding a slight accent, decrescendo on each note as in the pealing of the bells.

By ROLLO DILWORTH

Copyright © 2009 by HAL LEONARD CORPORATION
International Copyright Secured   All Rights Reserved

AUTUMN BREEZE

TIP: This warm-up focuses on the natural minor scale (*do re me fa so la te do*). Singers can strengthen their ability to sing the patterns *te so fa so* in Part I and *do me fa* in Part II. In Part II, the singers will have to differentiate between *me* (minor 3rd) versus *mi* (major 3rd). The goal is to sing with four measure phrases. Sing measures 7-10 with good expression, perhaps imitating the gentle autumn breeze. Part I is the "lead" line. Learn each line independently, and then combine.

Gently flowing and expressive (♩ = ca. 80)

By ROLLO DILWORTH

CELEBRATE PEACE

TIP: The class can first sing Part I alone, followed by Part II alone, and then combine the parts together. This is a good exercise for:
- using good breath control to sing phrases of varied lengths,
- dynamic expression,
- learning and performing articulation (accented staccato, tenuto and regular staccato),
- hearing solfege chromaticism (*te-la-le-so*),
- learning and performing the ostinato rhythm in Part II (eighth rest, two sixteenths, eighth).

By ROLLO DILWORTH

A SEASONAL BLUES

TIP: Use this warm-up to introduce or reinforce the following concepts:
- swing eighths,
- tenuto versus staccato,
- head voice "sighs,"
- descending glissando,
- syncopation (eighth, quarter, eighth),
- lowered pitches of the blues scales: *me* (lowered 3rd), *se* (lowered 5th) and *te* (lowered 7th).

With an expressive, bluesy swing (♩ = ca. 112)

By ROLLO DILWORTH

TOGETHER AS ONE

TIP: Use this warm-up to introduce or reinforce the following concepts:
- syncopation,
- imitation,
- intervals of seconds and fourths,
- unison versus harmony,
- tenuto versus staccato,
- solfege singing (especially *le* and *te*),
- phrasing and breath control (only breathing at the commas and periods),
- singing with expression (teacher chooses and adds dynamic markings).

By ROLLO DILWORTH

Copyright © 2010 by HAL LEONARD CORPORATION
International Copyright Secured   All Rights Reserved

OK TO REPRODUCE

A SOLFEGE SHOW

TIP: Use this warm-up to introduce or reinforce the following concepts:

- rhythm – quarter + eighth vs. eighth + quarter in 6/8 time,
- all intervals, except 7ths (chromatic half steps, 2nds, 3rds, 4ths, 5ths, 6ths),
- solfege syllables – *te* (lowered 7th) and *si* (raised 5th),
- diction,
- breath management and phrasing: singing two-bar phrases without taking a breath. As an extension, the descant people could experiment with singing four-bar phrases without taking a breath.

By ROLLO DILWORTH

Happily (♩. = ca. 52) *(4 measures introduction on recording)*

Descant *(2nd & 3rd times)*: Do — ti — la — te —

Melody *(1st & 3rd times)*: Gath - er the mu - sic, now hur - ry, let's go.

La so so do re do ti Te la do

Let's put to - geth - er a sol - fege show. Sing-ing songs that are new and

re mi do La so so do re do ti do (re mi)

songs that we know, like la la ti do so mi fa mi re do

A LITTLE LATIN SCATTIN'

TIP: Sing using scat syllables provided or using solfege ("la" based minor mode). Watch for the tenuto, staccato, and accented staccato articulations. Have students create their own scat syllables and percussion rhythms that match the rhythm patterns found in the music. The harmony part should be sung the second time through.

Spiritoso (♩ = ca. 96)

By ROLLO DILWORTH

WALKIN' IN BLUES COUNTRY

TIP: This exercise can be sung unison Part I or unison Part II, or both parts combined. Use this exercise when you want to explore the concepts of: tenuto, interval training of seconds, thirds or fourths, lowered seventh (*te*) versus the diatonic major seventh (*ti*). This piece can be sung with straight eighths or swung eights. Good diction is important!

By ROLLO DILWORTH

Bluesy (♩ = ca. 108)

WINTER MIX

TIP: For added reinforcement of mixed meter (6/8 versus 2/4), singers can walk the **microbeat** (tri-o-la, tri-o-la, ti ti, ti) then move to the **macrobeat** (dotted quarter, dotted quarter, quarter, quarter). The class can be divided into two groups (one group on the micro and one on the macro). The tenuto markings indicate syllabic stress. The singers should lighten up on the second measure of the words "play-ing" and "sway-ing." Students can play the open 5th bass parts on an Orff xylophone.

By ROLLO DILWORTH

Merrily (♩. = ca. 68)

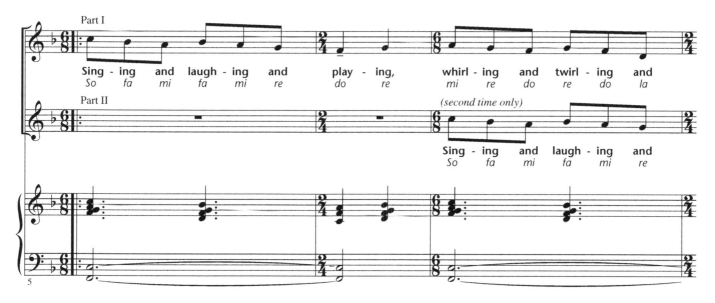

Part I

Sing - ing and laugh - ing and play - ing, whirl - ing and twirl - ing and
So fa mi fa mi re do re mi re do re do la

Part II

(second time only)

Sing - ing and laugh - ing and
So fa mi fa mi re

sway - ing, all a - cross the win - ter
so la so la do re mi fa

play - ing, whirl - ing and twirl - ing and sway - ing
do re mi re do re do la so la

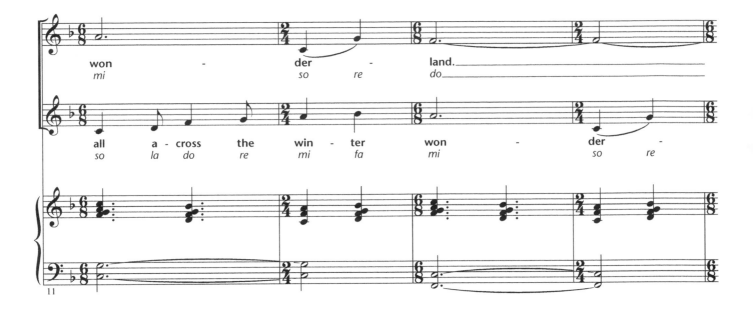

won - der - land. _____
mi   so re   do _____

all   a - cross the win - ter won - der -
so   la do   re   mi   fa   mi   so re

land. _____
do _____

RAINDROPS

TIP: Use this warm-up to address the following concepts:
- *do* to *so*,
- *do* to *la*,
- *so* to *do*,
- *fa* versus *fi*,
- staccato versus legato,
- singing the major scale,
- syllabic stress
  (e.g. on "rain" and "fall").

By ROLLO DILWORTH

A STAR IN THE NIGHT

TIP: Use this warm-up to address the following concepts:
- swing feel,
- skips (thirds),
- breath support for sustained pitches in descant,
- strive for tall vowels throughout,
- managing diphthongs (ah + ee),
- double consonants,
- stepwise motion,
- leaps (fourths and fifths).

With a moderate Swing (♩ = c. 100)

By ROLLO DILWORTH

NATURE SINGS

TIP: Use this warm-up to address the following concepts:
- syllabic stress (strong versus weak syllables), especially on the words "o-ver" and "un-der,"
- tenuto markings (support the stressed syllables),
- intervals: octaves, sixths, fourths, seconds (whole steps and half steps),
- *fa* versus *fi*,
- *la* versus *li* versus *le*,
- diction – the tapered "r" sound in the words "o-ver," "un-der" and "na-ture" (as opposed to the pirate "r" sound).

By ROLLO DILWORTH

MUSIC IN THE AIR

TIP: This exercise can be sung unison with just the melody or add the descant for a part-singing warm-up. This piece focuses on the following concepts:

• rhythms in 6/8 time (quarter + eighth, two sixteenths + eighth),
• diction – attacks with clean consonants and cut-offs on the rests with clean consonants,
• solfege, especially the sequence in the first two measures and the leaps of *do – so*, *do – la,* and *re – te.*

Consider adding this flexible Orff accompaniment option when using this warm-up for your vocal groups or general music classes. Any combination works!

Optional Orff Accompaniment

By ROLLO DILWORTH

MUSIC IN THE AIR

Joyfully (♩. = 56)

By ROLLO DILWORTH

A PATRIOT'S MARCH

TIP: This exercise can be sung unison with just Vocals 1 or add Vocals 2 for a part-singing warm-up. This piece focuses on the following concepts:
- steady beat,
- diction,
- solfege (stepwise motion, leading tone *ti* to *do*, skips of a third and a leap of *mi* to *la*,
- anacrusis (the sixteenth note pick up),
- add marching steps to the quarter note pulse.

Consider adding the flexible Orff and percussion accompaniment below when using this warm-up for your vocal groups or general music classes. Any combination works!

Optional Orff & Percussion Accompaniment

A steady March (♩ = 60)

By ROLLO DILWORTH

A PATRIOT'S MARCH

A steady March (♩ = 60)

By ROLLO DILWORTH

A WINTER DREAM

TIP: This exercise can be sung unison with just Voice 1, or add Voice 2 for a part-singing warm-up. This piece focuses on the following concepts:

- descending third (*do* to *la*),
- descending fourth (*la* to *mi*),
- descending fifth (*so* to *do*),
- *mi-re-do* versus *do-re-me* (lowered third),
- ascending minor third (*so* to *te* and *re* to *fa*),
- canon,
- diction (especially letters "f" and "c").

Consider adding the flexible Orff and percussion accompaniment below when using this warm-up for your vocal groups or general music classes. Any combination works!

Optional Orff & Percussion Accompaniment

Dreamy (♩. = 54)

By ROLLO DILWORTH

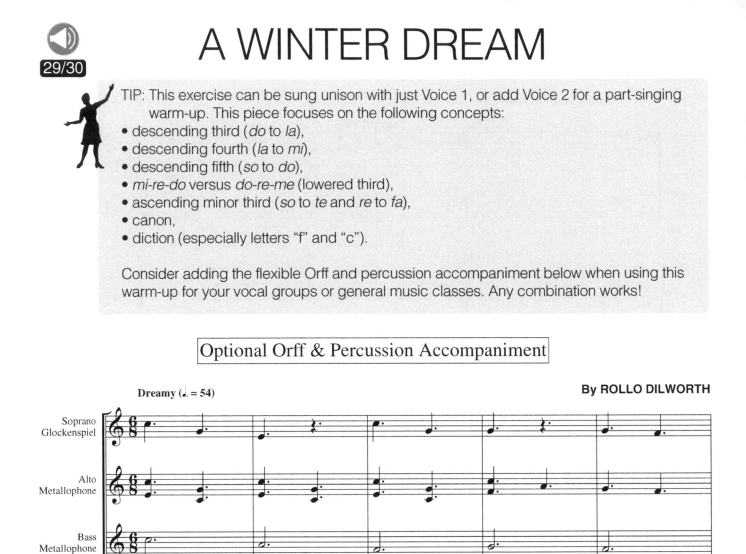

A WINTER DREAM

By ROLLO DILWORTH

TIME FOR CELEBRATION

TIP: This exercise can be sung unison with just Voice 1 or add Voice 2 for a part-singing warm-up. This piece focuses on the following concepts:
- *mi* to *so* (rising major third),
- *do* to *la* (descending minor third),
- stepwise motion (diatonic),
- diction (crisp consonants needed!),
- distinguishing between quarter note, two eighths, four sixteenths, and dotted eighth/sixteenth rhythms (through reading and performance).

Consider adding the flexible Orff and percussion accompaniment below when using this warm-up for your vocal groups or general music classes. Any combination works!

Optional Orff & Percussion Accompaniment

Joyously (♩ = 54)

By ROLLO DILWORTH

TIME FOR CELEBRATION

By ROLLO DILWORTH

SHINING STARS

TIP: This exercise can be sung unison with just Voice 1 or add Voice 2 for a part-singing warm-up. This piece focuses on the following concepts:

- various rhythm patterns in 6/8 time – eighth, eighth, rest; sixteenth, sixteenth, eighth, eighth;
- E minor tonality – e minor triad (*la* to *do*, *do* to *mi*, *mi* down to *la*); *la* to *do*, *la* to *te*;
- G major tonality – *do* to *so*;
- diction – double consonants (stars, shining); the objective is to quickly get to the vowel sound;

- final consonants (starS, shininG); the consonants should be released on the rests;
- syllabic stress – primary emphasis on syllables that fall on beat 1; secondary emphasis on syllables that fall on beat 4.

Consider adding the flexible Orff and percussion accompaniment below when using this warm-up for your vocal groups or general music classes.

Optional Orff & Percussion Accompaniment

With wonder and awe (♩. = 42)

By ROLLO DILWORTH

SHINING STARS

By ROLLO DILWORTH

HURRY UP

TIP: There are many concepts to explore in this warm-up exercise:
- canon/round,
- vocal timbre (change the vocal tone to sound like a clock on the "tick, tock, tick"),
- solfege (mainly stepwise motion; skips of *la* to *do* and *mi* to *so*; leaps of *so* to *do* and *re* to *la*),
- picardy third at the end (*re* to *di*),
- G minor versus B♭ major tonality,
- diction,
- syllabic stress (strong versus weak syllables; observe the tenuto marking on "fleeting" and "meeting"),
- facial expressions that should accompany this piece,
- improvisatory movement that could be performed (e.g. looking at one's wristwatch during the "tick, tock, tick" motive).

This piece can be repeated multiple times, each time getting faster.

Consider adding the flexible Orff and percussion accompaniment below when using this warm-up for your vocal groups or general music classes. Any combination works!

Optional Orff & Percussion Accompaniment

By ROLLO DILWORTH

HURRY UP

(4 measures introduction on recording)

With forward motion ($\quarternote = 60$)

By ROLLO DILWORTH

JAZZIN' IT UP

TIP: Use this warm-up to explore these concepts:
- legato versus staccato articulations,
- singing vocal jazz scat syllables,
- solfege syllables mi versus me (lowered third),
- singing a diminished triad (m. 7),
- swing eighths and triplets,
- solfege syllable *te* (lowered 7th in m. 4 of Voice 2).

Consider adding the flexible Orff, body percussion and claves accompaniment below when using this warm-up for your vocal groups or general music classes. Any combination works!

Optional Orff & Percussion Accompaniment

By ROLLO DILWORTH

JAZZIN' IT UP

(2 measures introduction on recording)

By ROLLO DILWORTH

Copyright © 2012 by HAL LEONARD CORPORATION
International Copyright Secured   All Rights Reserved

LET'S ROCK AND ROLL

TIP: Use this warm-up to explore these concepts:
- 2-part harmony,
- syncopation
- interval *so* to *fi* (in measure 7),
- clarity of diction (especially consonants at ends of words),
- tenuto marking on the word "Oh,"
- outline of tonic triad in vocals (m. 6),
- breath management and sustain of pitch in mm. 9–11.

Consider adding the flexible Orff and percussion accompaniment below when using this warm-up for your vocal groups or general music classes. Any combination works!

Optional Orff & Percussion Accompaniment

By ROLLO DILWORTH

LET'S ROCK AND ROLL

By ROLLO DILWORTH

SHINE YOUR LIGHT

TIP: Use this warm-up to explore these concepts:
- diphthong in the word "shine" – both "ah" and "ee" vowel sounds are present. Sustain the "ah" sound for as long as possible, articulate the second vowel sound "ee" upon the release or connection to next syllable.
- clarity of diction especially in sixteenth note passages,
- singing perfect fourths (*so* to *do* in m. 2; *mi* to *la* in m. 4; *la* to *re* in m. 10),
- altered scale degrees (*te* in m. 2; *fi* in m. 5),
- minor third (*re* to *fa* in m. 3) versus major third (*re* to *fi* in m. 5),
- rhythm patterns (dotted quarter and eighth; dotted quarter and sixteenth, sixteenth, eighth, sixteenth),
- syncopation.

Consider adding the flexible Orff and tambourine accompaniment below when using this warm-up for your vocal groups or general music classes. Any combination works!

Optional Orff & Percussion Accompaniment

By ROLLO DILWORTH

Joyfully (♩ = 80)

SHINE YOUR LIGHT

By ROLLO DILWORTH

WATCHING THE SKY

TIP: Use this warm-up to explore these concepts:
- C major triad (descending),
- C major scale,
- lowered 7th (*te*) in Part I,
- syncopation,
- perfect fourth interval (Part I, mm. 5–7),
- stressed versus unstressed syllables (especially in mm. 5-7),
- diction with diphthongs ("sky" in m. 1, "high" in m. 3 and "light" in m. 5).

The body percussion parts can all be handled by one person (or small ensemble in which everyone plays all parts).

Consider adding the flexible Orff and body percussion accompaniment below when using this warm-up for your vocal groups or general music classes. Any combination works!

Optional Orff & Body Percussion Accompaniment

By ROLLO DILWORTH

WATCHING THE SKY

By ROLLO DILWORTH

OFF THE BEATEN PATH

TIP: Use this warm-up to explore these concepts:
- syncopation,
- *te* versus *ti*,
- tonic triad,
- stepwise motion,
- descending minor 7th (*fa* to *so* in measure 12),
- observing quarter rests (in Voice 2),
- ascending fourths (*so* to *do*; *do* to *fa*),
- descending fourths (*re* to *la*).

Consider adding the flexible Orff and percussion accompaniment below when using this warm-up for your vocal groups or general music classes. Any combination works!

Optional Orff & Percussion Accompaniment

By ROLLO DILWORTH

OFF THE BEATEN PATH

By ROLLO DILWORTH

HIDE AND SEEK

TIP: Use this warm-up to explore these concepts:
- minor mode (natural),
- singing the minor triad,
- diction (clean, crisp consonants!),
- rhythms (4 sixteenths, two sixteenths and eight, eight and two sixteenths),
- maintaining tall "ah" space while singing high E's in top voice part
  (on the words "hiding," "where," "soon," and "and"),
- perfect fourth (*so* to *do*) in measures 4–5 (lower part),
- perfect fourth (*mi* to *la*) in measures 8–9 (lower part).

Consider adding the flexible Orff and percussion accompaniment below when using this warm-up for your vocal groups or general music classes. Any combination works!

Optional Orff & Percussion Accompaniment

By ROLLO DILWORTH

HIDE AND SEEK

By ROLLO DILWORTH

ABOUT THE WRITER

Rollo A. Dilworth is Associate Professor of Choral Music Education at Temple University's Boyer School of Music in Philadelphia, PA. In addition to teaching undergraduate and graduate courses in choral music education, he conducts the University Chorale. Prior to his appointment at Temple, Dilworth served as Director of Choral Activities and Music Education at North Park University in Chicago, IL for 13 years. He earned a Doctorate degree in Conducting Performance at Northwestern University and he holds undergraduate and graduate degrees from Case Western Reserve University and the University of Missouri – St. Louis, respectively.

An award-winning composer and active conductor, educator and clinician, Rollo has taught choral music at all levels and has conducted numerous all-state and honor choirs. In addition to the arrangements and original choral works he has published with Hal Leonard, he is also a contributing author for *Essential Elements for Choir, Experiencing Choral Music,* and for John Jacobson's *Music Express.* He is the author of *Choir Builders: Fundamental Vocal Techniques for Classroom and General Use.* In addition to composing music in the choral genre, his research interests are in the areas of African-American music, global indigenous folk music traditions, and music education curriculum and instruction.